THE BODY PARTS MENU
OF GOOD
TABLE MANNERS

ISBN 1515375226

Why I wrote this book

If you come from a part of the world where Western table manners appear cumbersome and mysterious, you will be grateful for this book's simplicity.

If you live in the western world, you may be puzzled by the number of ways people hold their utensils, and wonder what is really correct, since everyone thinks their way is the right way.

Table manners define the meaning of a meal. Eating is simply a physical need, but dining is a social ritual.

Though the rules of table manners are constantly changing, and are as varied as cultures, they share one rule: well-mannered people eat "pretty."

This book describes what is considered pretty in the Western world and cautions about possible blunders.

Enjoy!

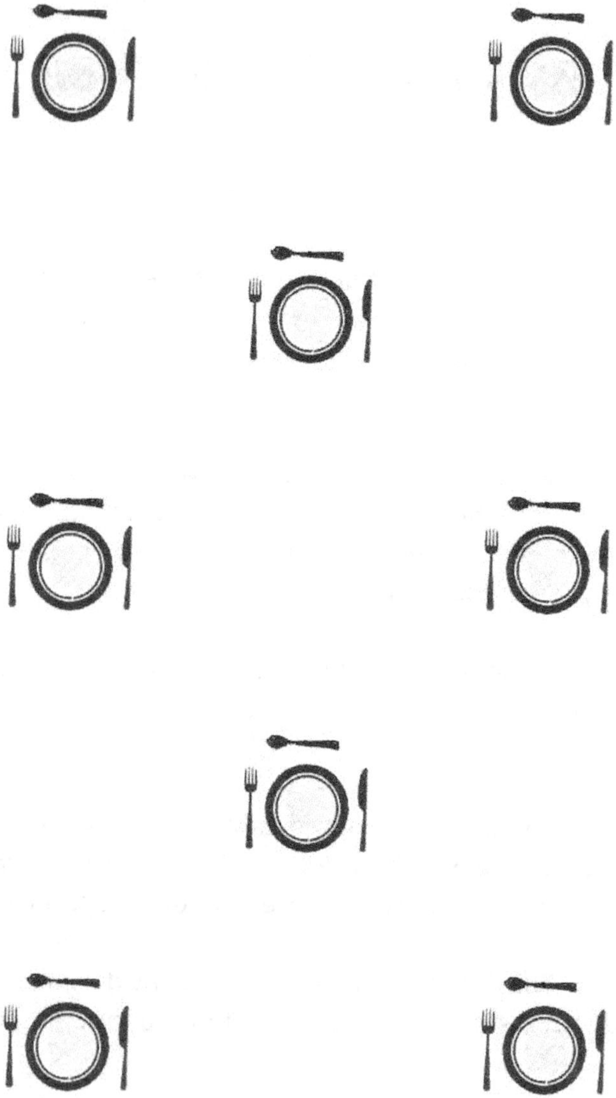

THE BODY PARTS
MENU
OF GOOD
TABLE MANNERS

A Sure-Fire
Survival Guide
For the Western World

Dagmar F. Pelzer, Ed.D.

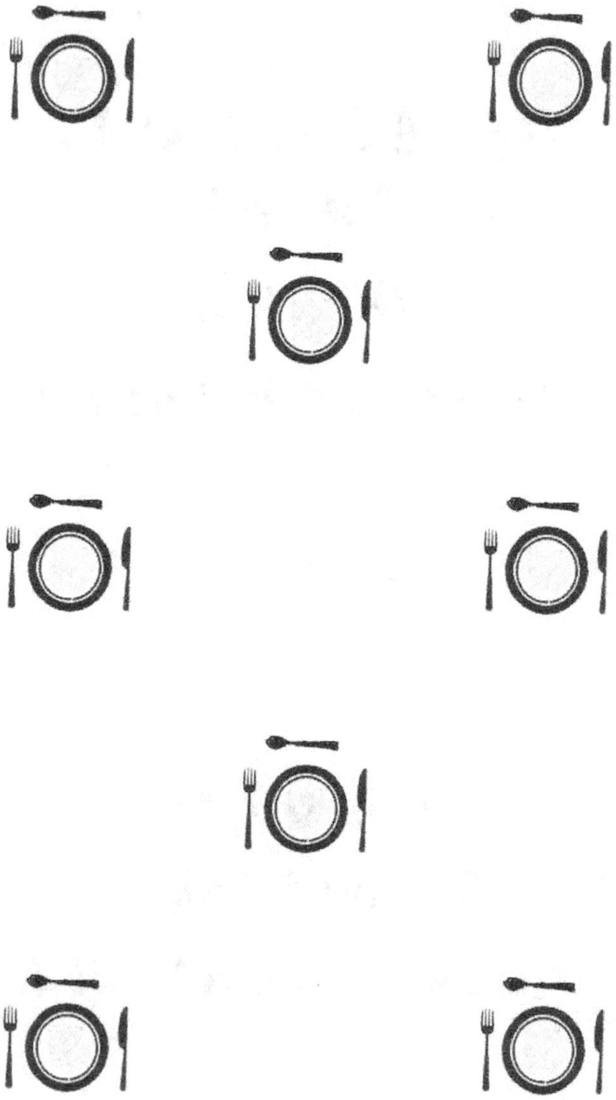

To my mother, grandmother,
and great-aunts
Who worked so tirelessly

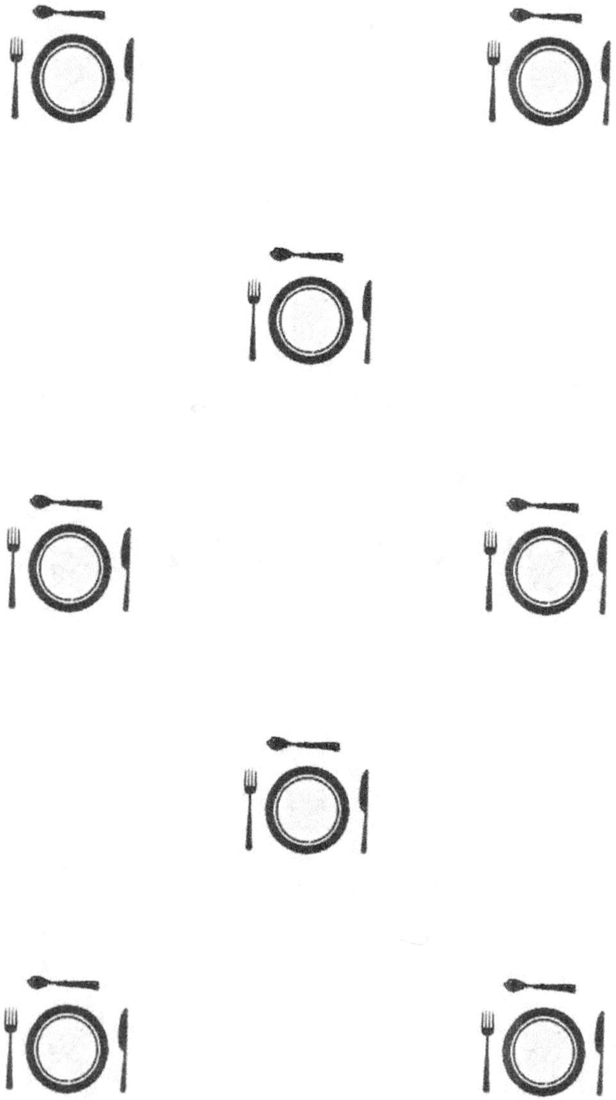

Acknowledgments

J want to thank my friends, fellow diners (known and unknown) and all their implicit and direct suggestions for writing this book.

Special thanks to the Dr. Phil Show! Years ago one of his guests complained about her husband's bad table manners. Dr. Phil advised her to tell him to go and get some. Having observed many people with really bad manners, this show encouraged me to look for a simple book on table manners. After various unsuccessful searches, I wrote to the Dr. Phil Show and asked for recommendations. No answer. Weeks later I wrote again, still no answer. Never an answer.

The need for simple instructions kept bothering me. My good friend, Rose White, kept insisting that I write a short and easy to follow guide.

Amanda Castleman, teacher of wonderful travel writing courses, I love you forever. Wouldn't have accomplished this without your editing, help, and encouragement!

And finally, I have to admit that I should have listened to Tony Thomas, my dearly beloved, who early on advised me to use templates for the layout. It would have saved me lots of headaches and time.

Table of Contents

Chapter 3

What do you do with that stuff on the table?

Chapter 4

Pass me something, please!

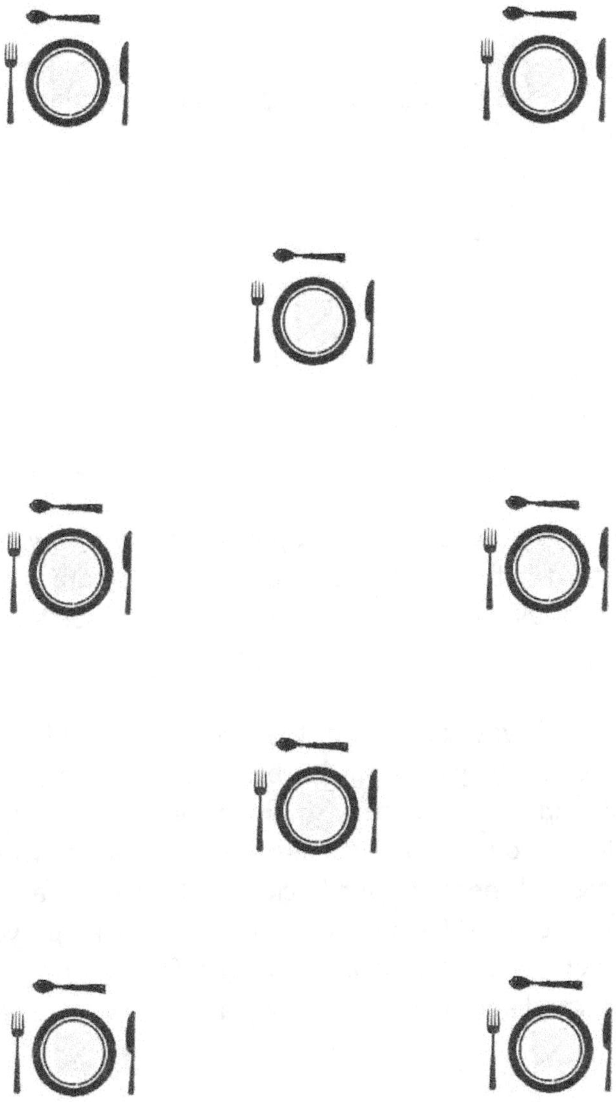

Introduction

*I*f you come from a part of the world where Western table manners appear cumbersome and mysterious, you will be grateful for our book's simplicity.

*I*f you are from the western world, and someone has given you this book as a present, they either know us, or they're signaling your manners could improve. Don't be insulted. Save that for when people talk behind your back and drop hints about poor etiquette (or worse). Anyone who helps you sharpen your table manners is a real friend, one truly concerned about your social well-being!

Previously, no simple books existed on dining basics for adults. I found instructions or books for teens and children that could be insulting if given to adults. Many books describe complicated table settings that include multiple spoons, various forks and knives, and a crystal forest of glasses. We don't need all that. We are normal people, not royalty. Should we get to the aristocratic level, we'll make sure to learn how to behave there too.

Part I consists of a list the killing behaviors, the ones that could mess up your lives. I call them the Seven Mortal Sins of Dining.

Part II, the most important part of the book, is my approach to table manners via body parts: where your arms and hands should be, how you should hold your head, where to put your butt, and what to do with your hands and feet.

In Part III I share why we have table manners, where they originated, and how they have changed over the years.

Part IV lists frequently asked questions.

Part V consists of two stories, one on bravery, and another on great embarrassment and humiliation.

Learn, live and enjoy!

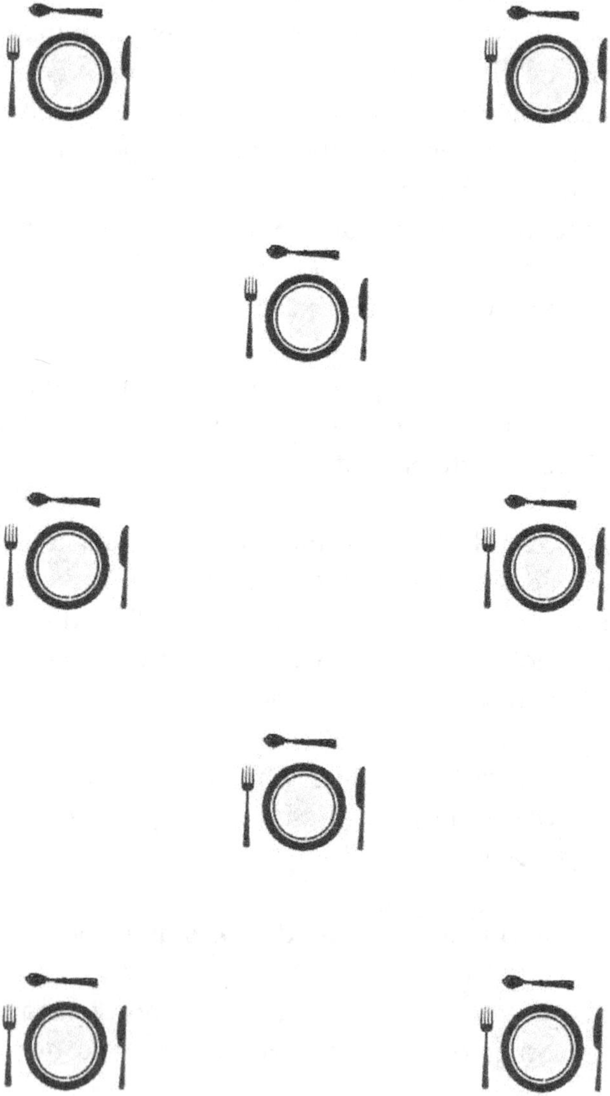

Chapter 1

Ten Mortal Sins of Dining to avoid

They

Could

Cost

You

A potential job offer

Promotion

Second date

Repeat invitation

Inclusion in professional events

MORTAL SIN 1

Placing arm in front of plate

NEVER!

MORTAL SIN 2

Leaning elbows on table while eating

NEVER!

MORTAL SIN 3

Loading soup and ce-real spoon so full it spills over

NEVER

MORTAL SIN 4

Leaving mouth im-print on glass or cup
(with or without lipstick)

NEVER!

MORTAL SIN 5

Chewing with mouth open

NEVER!

MORTAL SIN 6

Speaking with mouth full

NEVER!

MORTAL SIN 7

Picking teeth at the table

NEVER!

MORTAL SIN 8

Using fingers to push food on to fork or spoon

NEVER!

MORTAL SIN 9

Scratching or rubbing head, nose, or face

NEVER!

MORTAL SIN 10

Keeping face perma-nently bowed over plate

NEVER!

Chapter 2

Where should your body parts be?

Dining should be like walking. Automatic, without thinking about the rules.

When you walk down the street, you don't check how your left foot crosses the right one, if you point your toes in or out. You quickly scan the path ahead and continue your conversation with your companion or thoughts. You learned to walk, and the rules of walking when you were little. You were cautioned by your parents or guardians, and you learned. In time you applied your walking skills to running, jumping, and climbing.

Dining is no different. Your good table manners should be as automatic as walking. No need to think about holding fork and knife, where to keep arms and legs, how not to spill stuff. Observe others when a new food, glass, or dish, are unfamiliar. And then you can even ask.

It's all really easy when your body parts are trained do all the work.

Butt and chest

On a chair, your bottom should sit snugly against the back of the seat. Lean your elbows against the sides of your body: only your hands and wrists should rest on the table's surface. Move your chair inwards, if need be. But don't scratch it over the floor! Lift up your rump a little and scoot your seat with two hands. The same goes when you get up.

In a booth, you can lean back until your dinner arrives. Then shift forward until the distance between your chest and the table is the same as if you were sitting on a chair.

Head

When you eat, your head is like the stiff extension of your back. Yes, you look down to your food and pick it up with the appropriate utensil (which can include your fingers). But then, on your unslumped shoulders, your head is bought forward as you bend forward from your butt. As you approach your plate, the chin rises up a bit to parallel the table, and the utensil with the food goes into your mouth, tines or tip of spoon straight in, never from the side. This is a good way to observe what others do, to see who's talking, paying attention to what they're saying, and to make eye contact.

By looking at people while you are dining, you are participating in thought exchanges, you are conversing!

Can't do that when you're focusing exclusively on the food on your plate!

Back

Your back should always be straight, all the way up to the head. Of course, you bend your head to look around or to serve yourself. But when you eat, keep your spine stacked in a vertical column and lean forward slightly over your plate. Extend your chin a bit so that you have an easy line between your food and your mouth. Once you've taken a bite, shift back into your original position.

Please note that you can lean against the back of a chair, but not the back of a booth. You just have to suffer and sit straight. The exception is when you take a break between courses or rest between too many bites. Then you can place your utensils on your plate – preferably criss-cross, but never on the table or tablecloth – and relax. When you're ready to continue your meal, go into the straight position again, pick up your utensils, and continue to eat. And please, don't slump!

Forearms

Between courses, or after you have finished your meal, you may – and this is part of the more relaxed manners – place your hands up to the middle of your forearms on the table.

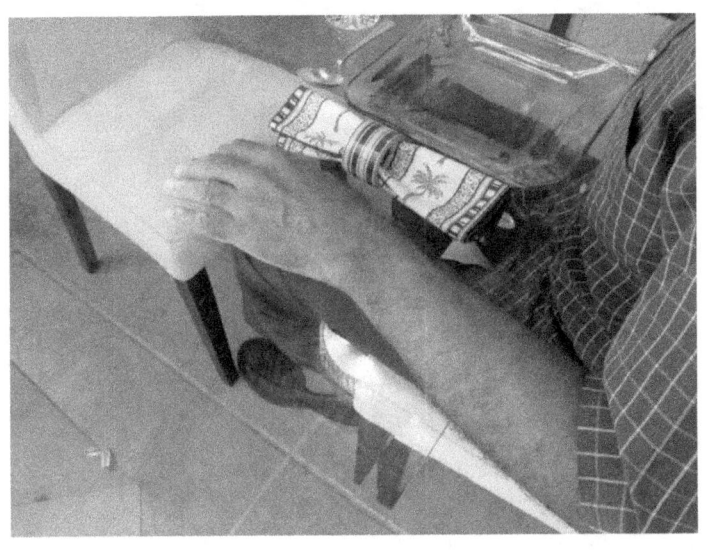

Hands

Your hands can rest on the table up to your wrists, and no further. You may place your left hand on your lap, but it is more common to keep it next to the plate. If you have eaten something with your fingers, please wipe them on your napkin on your lap before touching anything.

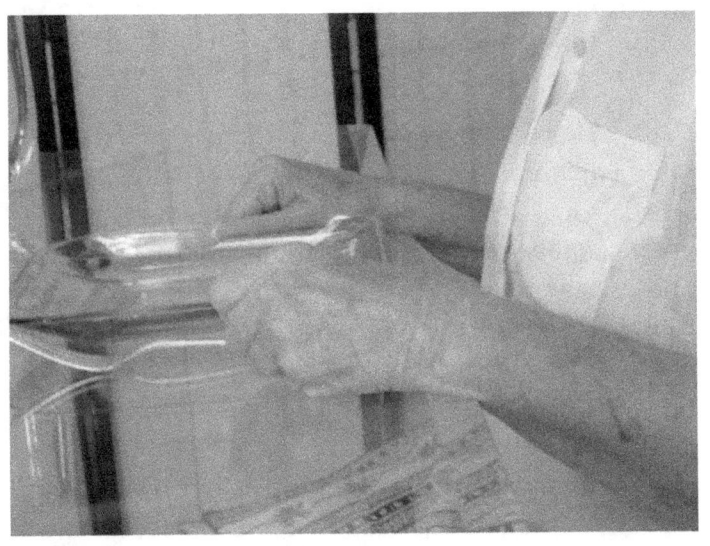

Elbows

There is absolutely no room for elbows on the table while you eat. Never, ever. From elbow to the wrist, your arm shouldn't touch the table while you're dining. No elbow or arm in front of the plate and no perching on or against the table. And never prop up your chin: you're not taking senior photos or posing for a dust jacket, after all.

Elbows should remain near the body, especially when people are seated close to each other. Nobody loves getting their space invaded, let alone being jabbed or bumped.

When you've finished your meal and the plates have been removed, you may place your elbows on the table if you really want to.

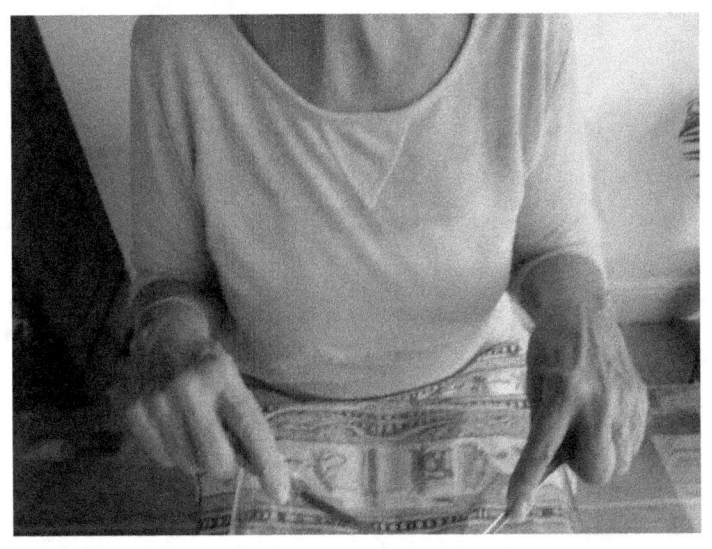

Lap

While you eat, your napkin should be open or at least half open on your lap, with your feet and knees pressed together.

Some people who eat with the fork in their right hand (an American habit) keep their left hand under the table. Though not every culture does this, people generally understand the tradition varies.

While you are waiting for food, or after you have finished your meal, you may keep your hands on your lap.

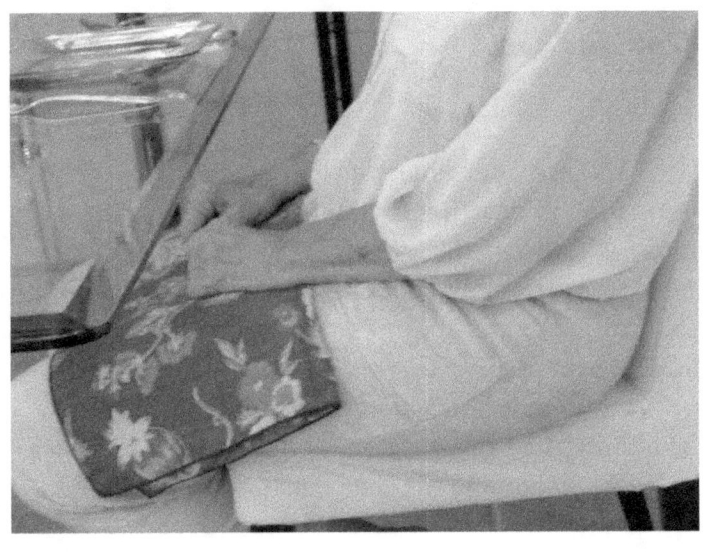

Legs and feet

Place your knees next to each other with your feet under them. Don't stretch, spread or cross your legs: the person across from you or next to you needs space too. And for heaven's sake, don't play "kneesies" or "footsies," unless you're seated next to your partner. Even bumping your neighbor accidentally can be interpreted as an intrusion or flirtation, and a short "I'm sorry," acknowledging the faux pas is appropriate.

You don't ever want to be embarrassed when your neighbor has to ask you to keep your knees or feet to yourself.

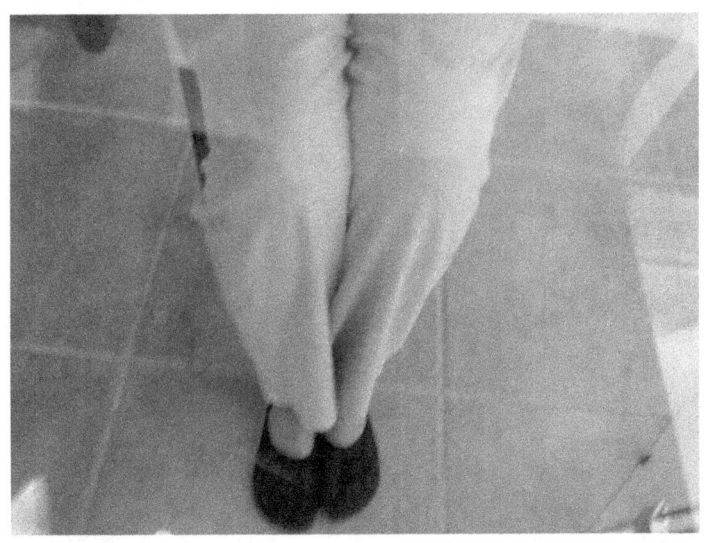

Chapter 3

What do you do with that stuff on the table?

When you hold your stemmed glass correctly, you show that you know about wine. When you eat finger food with ease, don't fumble with your utensils and treat your napkin with dignity, you define yourself as a person in the know. It takes just a little bit of learning and practice to be comfortable anywhere.

Napkins

*T*he table may be set with paper or cloth napkin on the plate lying down, standing up in decorative formation, or lounging next to the fork on the left side. Imitate your host as to when you move the serviette to your lap. If you are in a restaurant, transfer it when you sit down, if the waiter doesn't oblige first. Don't tuck it into your shirt! Only lobster bibs belong around your neck.

*B*efore you drink, bring your napkin to your mouth and dab it, so that you don't leave any kind of ring on the glass or cup. Your mouth print on a glass or cup looks unattractive. A lipstick impression doesn't read "pretty" either! If you wear lipstick, discretely blot your lips with a tissue before dinner to make sure the color doesn't smear all over the linens.

*J*f you leave the table for any reason, either place your napkin folded casually on the left side of your plate or on your seat. Do not crumple it!

*L*eave your napkin on your lap until everyone has finished dining.

Cutlery

Customs vary from culture to culture, and even within the same country. Often, there is no right or wrong.

Some things may look and feel awkward. It is up to the individual to try and imitate the hosts or not. For example, people brought up with a lefthand fork and righthand knife (common in Europe) may feel clumsy and uncomfortable transferring their fork to their right hand like many Americans. Some victories just aren't worth the struggle...

It is OK to ask for a knife, when you need one. Sometimes you find duplicated utensils around your plate. Always use the ones on the outside first. Place them on the plate from which you eat, and they will be picked up by a waiter or handed to the host and taken away. If uncertain, watch how others do it.

Spoons and Forks

Grasp your spoon as you would a pencil or pen. Hold your fork the same way if you hold its tines up, or you clasp them as you would a knife when cutting a loaf of bread. Leave an inch of space between your fingers and the part with which you eat.

Forks and Knives

Hold your knife as if you were cutting a loaf of bread, and grasp your fork the same way if you eat with the tines down, or when you're holding on to the food to be cut. Leave an inch of space between your fingers and the part with which you cut or eat.

Stubborn Food

Sometimes that morsel just won't climb on your fork or spoon. Never use your fingers! Use your knife or a teaspoon to give it a push. If you're on the dessert course and you only have one fork or spoon available, ask for another. Now you can push.

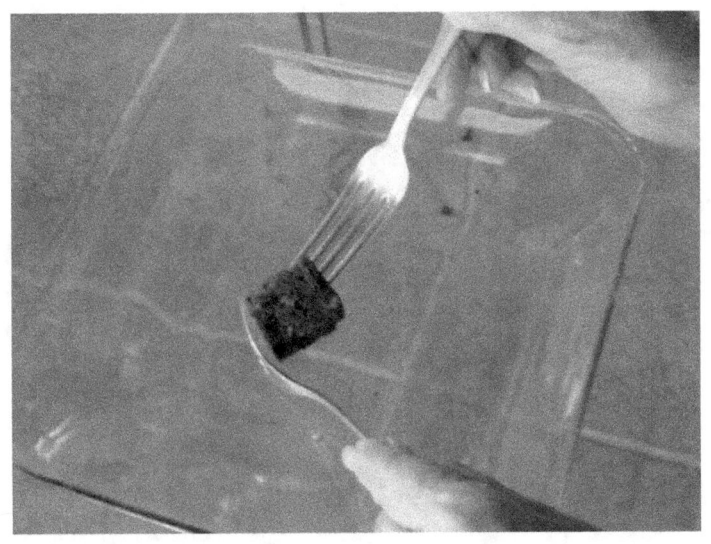

During a Meal

your utensils are not clean after you have had them in your mouth. Maybe some food particles have clung to them. Never put utensils back on the table or that beautiful tablecloth and leave stains! Rest them on the side of your plate.

Leaving the Table

When you leave the table but want to communicate that you aren't finished with your food, cross your knife and fork.

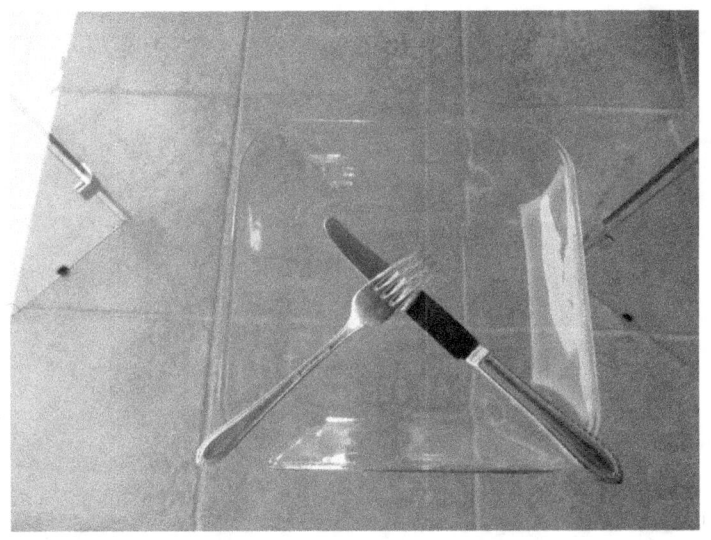

At the end of the meal

When you're finished with your meal, place your utensils in the 10 – 4 position.

Glasses

You hold a wine glass by the stem. Period. There is no grasping it anywhere else, especially if you want a toast to chime. When you toast, you take a sip. If you don't, it is considered an insult.

Unless....

Some cultures have exceptions, however. If companions toast you, then you don't drink. You just hold up the glass and thank them. You sit out that round, and then can tipple a bit later. People traveling for business or ceremonies should brush up on regional nuances like this – and always passing the port to the left in England – before departing.

Plates

Your plate belongs in front of you, one inch from the edge of the table, all through your meal, including when you have finished eating. Your waiter will remove it, your host will collect it, but please don't set or move it to the side. Not nice!

When multiple plates are used, watch your host and neighbors.

Finger food

Some foods may be eaten with your fingers, like bacon, fried chicken, French fries, tacos and hors d'oeuvres, to name just a few. Your fingertips will most likely get greasy. Before you pick up a utensil or glass, please wipe your fingers on your napkin under the table. This avoids leaving ugly spots on the cloth or tabletop.

In European countries people eat most everything with fork and knife, including pizza, fruit and open-faced sandwiches. So watch what your host, or others in a restaurant do, and follow suit. That said, if you find it difficult to handle tacos or a hamburger with fork and knife, it's better to be comfortable and fed, rather than proper and hungry.

Chapter 4

Pass me something

Responding to a simple request to pass a dish, utensil, napkin, or to pour wine for your neighbor, or maybe for everyone at the table is part of the package that is good table manners.

Sometimes, no waiter is around to tend to everyone's needs, or you're at someone's house where the host or hostess aren't going to act as waiters. Passing food incorrectly could turn into a big embarrassing spill or worse yet, make food turn inedible for some faint-hearted people.

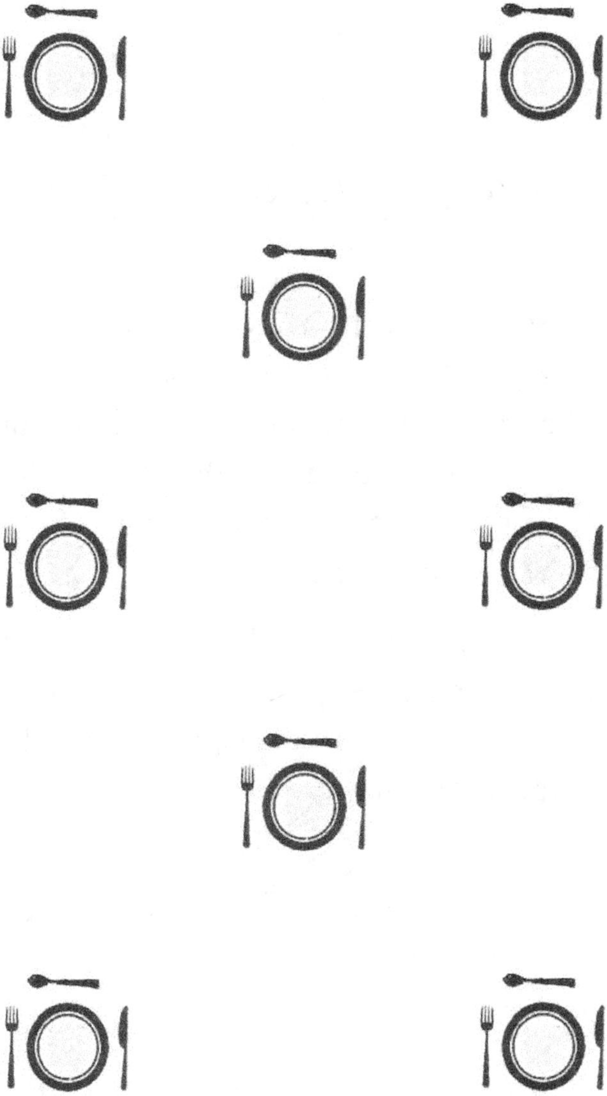

Pass me the fork, please.

Never pick up a fork or spoon by the tip, the part that holds the food and takes it to the mouth. Euuuuu, how unsanitary! Would you want to eat with it? Most likely you'd use your napkin to wipe it off. And never pick up a knife by its blade.

Always pick utensils up by the upper part of their handles. Then turn the tip towards you so that the recipient can take it from you comfortably.

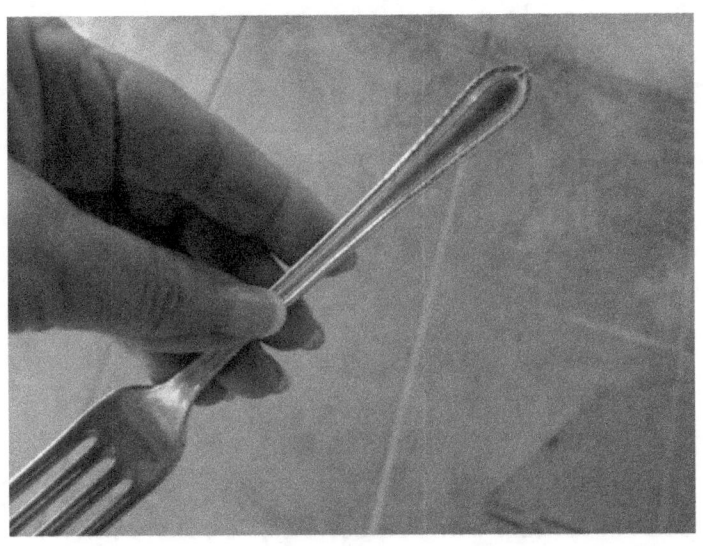

Pass me the pasta, please.

*T*hat big bowl of pasta is near you, and some-one the across the table from you would like for you to pass it over.

Use both hands, and leave enough space for the other person to take from you just below the rim. No thumbs inside the bowl, please. You could get burned. And you don't want to eat food that has been in contact with someone else's body, even if it's "just" a thumb.

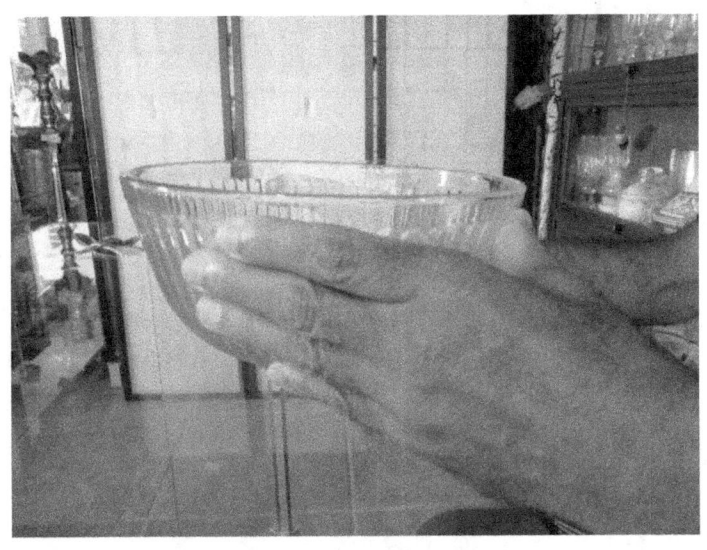

Pour the wine, please.

In most western cultures, wine is considered the crowning touch of a wonderful meal. Volumes of books are written on what wine to serve with what dish.

You not only serve the correct wine with white, red, or no meat, but you also pour it correctly.

There are several types of wine bottles, from regular 750 ml to big 1.5 liter. On some occasions you may be served wine in a decanter or in a round or oblong bottle with or without a handle. Whatever the shape and size, never ever pick up a bottle by the neck. It's not a chicken you're about to choke!

The small bottle is picked up with one hand in the middle of its body. It is also poured with one hand.

*L*arge bottles are picked up with one hand and supported with the other. Pick it up by the shoulder, that part between the body and the neck, and support it from the bottom with the other. Large bottles are usually quite heavy, and you pour just as you picked up, with both hands.

*J*f the decanter has a handle, pick it by the hands. Depending on weight and size, you support it with the other hand.

*A*n odd-shaped bottle is up for grabs. If light, pick it up as you would a small bottle, if heavy, use both hands.

How full do you fill the glasses?

Fill them just to the imaginary half full line if you're pouring red wine, and a little bit higher for white wine. Never fill glasses up to the top. And never "top off" wine, unless the recipient asks you to.

Chapter 5

Generally Speaking

*J*t's all about aesthetics. Every living being eats. From fleas to snow leopards to us at the top of food chain, we all need fuel. But there's nothing tidy about a predator ripping into a kill. Even angora goats – considered the tidiest eaters in the animal kingdom – don't worry about smudging their mohair.

*W*e factor this in with our cats and dogs and other pets, providing special mats and bowls to avoid messes. We expect animals to slobber and smear a bit. But debris from other people, who should know better, is another matter entirely. Think of your host who has to clean up after you, and his or her dismay over those deep stains setting into the tablecloth, maybe ruining it permanently. Do you really want to cause that type of discomfort? Humans invented etiquette to avoid ugliness. "Manners aim to facilitate life, to get rid of impediments," wrote Ralph Waldo Emerson in his 1844 essay on the topic. "They aid our dealing and conversation, as a railway aids travelling, by getting rid of all avoidable obstructions of the road."

*S*o, first, let's lay down some ground rules. "Please" and "thank you" go a long way. Lean in. Avoid leaving gobs of food on your silverware or mouth-prints on the rims of glassware. While it's fine to enjoy your dinner, no one needs to see how the sausage got made... Discretely wield your napkin to keep the table looking elegant, even as the meal progresses.

*D*on't stir and chop food around your plate, even if you're trying to conceal a small appetite. This doesn't fool anyone: it just looks unappetizing. Ask for a "no-thank-you" portion – and claim circumstances forced you into a big meal earlier – if you must. But don't turn the chef's hard work into unrecognizable hash.

*N*ever take more that you can eat. Whether you are handed bowls, have a host serve you, or dine buffet-style, don't let your plate get overloaded. Accept just a little of each dish. You can always agree to seconds later – the highest compliment to the chef in many cultures! Plus, it is no longer fashionable to leave food on your plate. If you are invited to someone's home, your hosts may mourn all the effort they put into food they have to (ewwwww!) scrape off your plate. So try not to leave any.

*E*xcept in a crisis, don't get up from the table to use the restroom. Visit at home or when you first arrive.

*T*urn off your mobile phone. Do not make or accept calls or respond to texts during a meal – or even Google a point being debated (unless requested). Diverting your attention is downright rude. If you're dealing with an emergency, inform your host ahead of time. Then politely excuse yourself to attend to matters in another room or outside.

*Y*ou may wonder what to do if you're plagued by allergies or just don't like something. Your host will be happy to accommodate special food requirements, but you need deal with your dislikes. If the invitation specifies a crickets-in-chocolate dinner and you just can't handle crickets in chocolates, don't accept the invitation. If your host asks if you eat her special delicacy, you can honestly answer "no", and the menu will   surprise you with something you can eat. But if you accept the invitation to feast on crickets, then hold your breath and eat them.

*C*ompliment your host on a wonderful dinner, a beautiful table, recognize effort, hard work, and time. You will be appreciated.

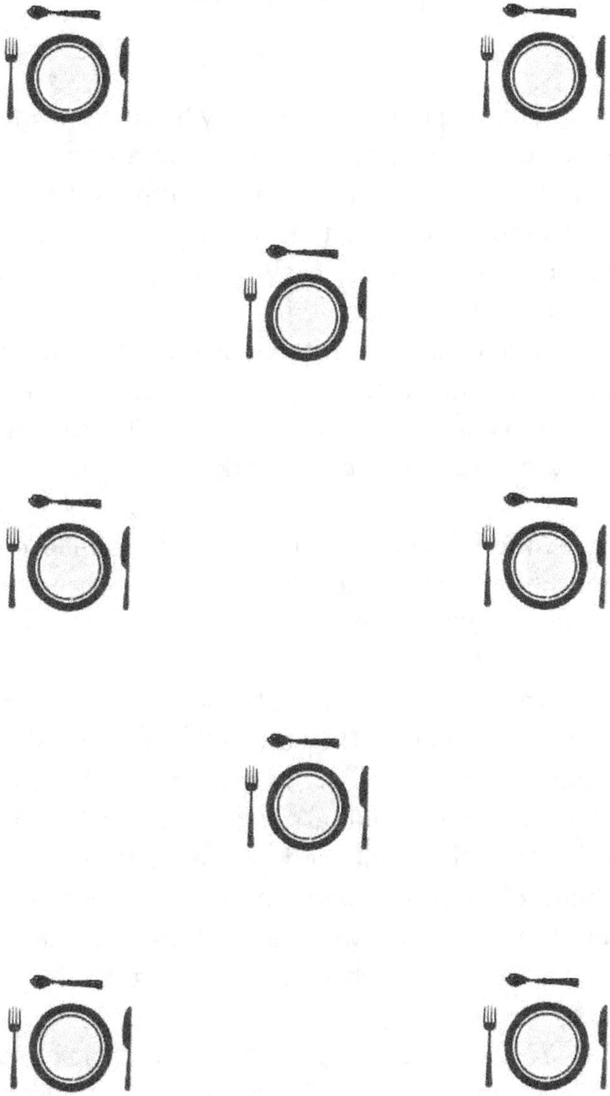

Of Course, History

What we find pretty or ugly has been evolving ever since groups of people sat – or sprawled – down together to share a meal. In the fifth century B.C. before modern toilets, the ancient Greeks brought poop pots to festivities. They not only used them at the table, but they sometimes ended drunken arguments by flinging the contents at the object of their displeasure. The custom of chamber pots was eventually transmitted to the Romans. These rather handy vessels became great works of art.

Other dining customs included public overeating and throwing up. The odor of all this must have been really delightful.

Regular people did not have individual plates until the middle ages. They ate with their hands from one bowl or platter in the middle of the table. Children usually were not allowed at the table. They stood behind the adults and caught what was tossed to them, often in competition with the dogs. At the end of the meal, they were allowed to scoop the last bits of food from the pots with their fingers.

In the 1700s people started transferring food from common bowls and platters onto their own plates. Traveling men always brought their own.

Forks went mainstream just few hundred years ago. In the eleventh century, an Italian princess was censured by the church because the utensil was an affront to God's intention for fingers.

The French court considered them dangerous. For hundreds of years, the two-pronged fork was used to pick plums and other small fruits out of their syrupy sauce.

In the early 1600s, the renowned English traveler Thomas Coryat returned from Italy with the practical table fork and was thoroughly ridiculed. "Fingers are for eating, not forks!" But within years Charles I of England declared that "it is decent to use a fork." This marked the beginning of modern table manners.

In the 1700s, a hundred years after England's nobility accepted forks, it became fashionable for the masses to have clean hands, and forks finally arrived.

The first table fork arrived in America a quarter century later. It was a gift to John Winthrop, governor of the Massachusetts Bay Colony. He found it so precious that he kept in in a leather pouch. Still, trends spread slowly back then, and Americans didn't even adopt the now-ubiquitous fork until the 1800s.

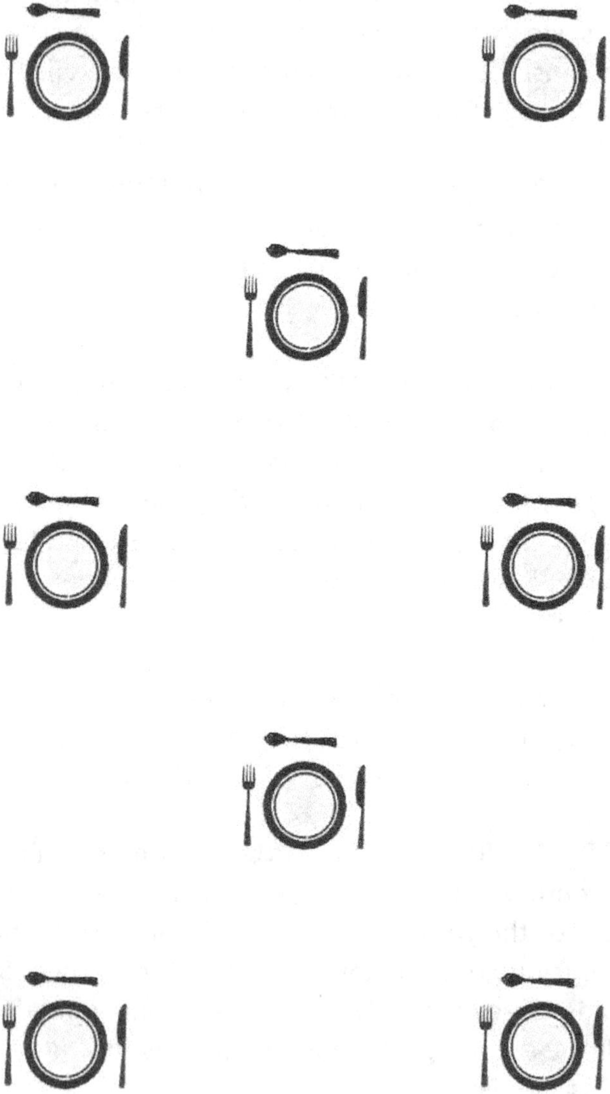

Relaxation of Strict Table Manners

The Western hemisphere's nobility and upper classes are still strict about their often cumbersome rituals: how many forks and knives are placed where, how many glasses should be placed on an elegant table, how napkins are folded or molded become important issues.

The non-nobility has become more relaxed, unless they really want to imitate nobility. Trends and customs change with need and perception.

For a while, it was fashionable to leave some food on the plate. This proved the diner wasn't starving. He or she had escaped from poverty. Now, we finish what's on our plates when we're guests in someone's house or when we eat at a buffet. The exception is a too-large serving delivered on a plate at a restaurant. But for that we have take-homes.

As recent as 20 years ago, children were forced to eat everything parents put in front of them. Now they can choose, oftentimes the worse for their health. Some adults have graduated to urging small tastes to introduce their offspring to unfamiliar food without a scene.

Our early forefathers and —mothers ate with their fingers. In the 1900s, especially in Europe, touching food with fingers meant low class or no class. Fast food killed that. Even in elegant restaurants, some foods are eaten or held with fingers: fried chicken, lobster, French fries, pizza, tacos, even bacon. Revolutionary!

Disputes arose if there should be a correct standard of behavior. Some held that the left hand needed to rest on one's lap, others said "no, it needs to be on the table." They debated what could be eaten with fingers and where guests should be seated.

Today, we're relaxed. Too much travel, too many cultures, too many habits. People from varied dining etiquette can peacefully come together for a meal, with everyone adhering to the manners of their own culture and upbringing. But, no matter where they are from, well-mannered people tend to eat "pretty," paying attention to the attractiveness of the settings, plating and comportment. An eye for beauty – and genuine gratitude for the hosts' effort – goes a long way, right around the globe.

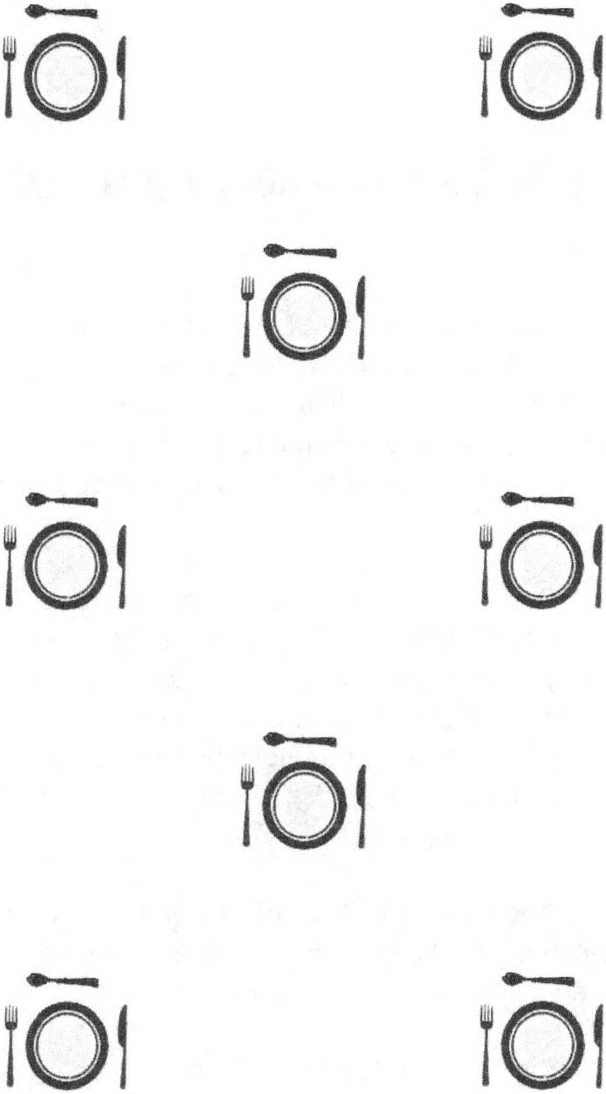

Who judges our table manners?

Everyone who sits down with you for a meal has an opinion on your style. So do yourself – and your parents or guardians, by extension – proud! Otherwise, poor table manners could cost you a second date, an invitation to network, or even a job or business deal.

But, remember, manners are relative. Your family's traditions may not apply in the regions or circles you wind up moving in. So stop, look, and listen. Mimic where you can. Or, if you can leave your shyness behind, ask your neighbor to demonstrate using an unfamiliar utensil. They will be delighted and enjoy helping you.

And take advantage of any etiquette training suggested by colleagues or employers: they're probably encouraging it for a reason....

The rules used to be rigid. They no longer are, fortunately. It just has to look nice.

Summary

Looking elegant

While flourishes exist, here are a few basic rules to always look elegant.

1- Take small bites, chew, swallow, talk. Don't lecture during a meal, your food will get cold. Whatever you have to say will be said eventually. Dining is supposed to be relaxing.

2- Don't "speak" with your utensils. If you gesture for emphasis, place your cutlery on your plate, and talk with your hands. Don't wave sharp and dirty objects around.

3- If you hold the fork in your right hand to eat and cross it over to your left to cut items, slice just one bite at a time. Don't carve up everything and make your food look like a battlefield (so unappetizing to your neighbors!). If, in the process, food sticks to your knife, slide both sides of the blade over the edge of the fork, then consume those morsels before continuing.

4-   The tips of your utensils must always be angled down towards the plate, whether the tines of your fork point up or down. This goes for spoons as well.

6-   Fill your soup or cereal spoon only 50 to 75 percent. You don't want the liquid to run off your spoon. Also, most cultures frown on slurping. Avoid it unless your homework indicates it's a compliment to the chef.

7-   Never place a used utensil on the table or tablecloth. If you are taking a pause during a meal, criss-cross your fork and knife. When you are finished eating, place the silverware in the 4 o'clock position.

At the end of the day, it really isn't hard to eat elegantly and correctly. Practice, and you will be a welcome guest wherever you may go. In a different culture, or when you're uncertain, watch how others do it, or ask.

Enjoy your food, enjoy your friends, and enjoy great conversations, and enjoy being invited again and again.

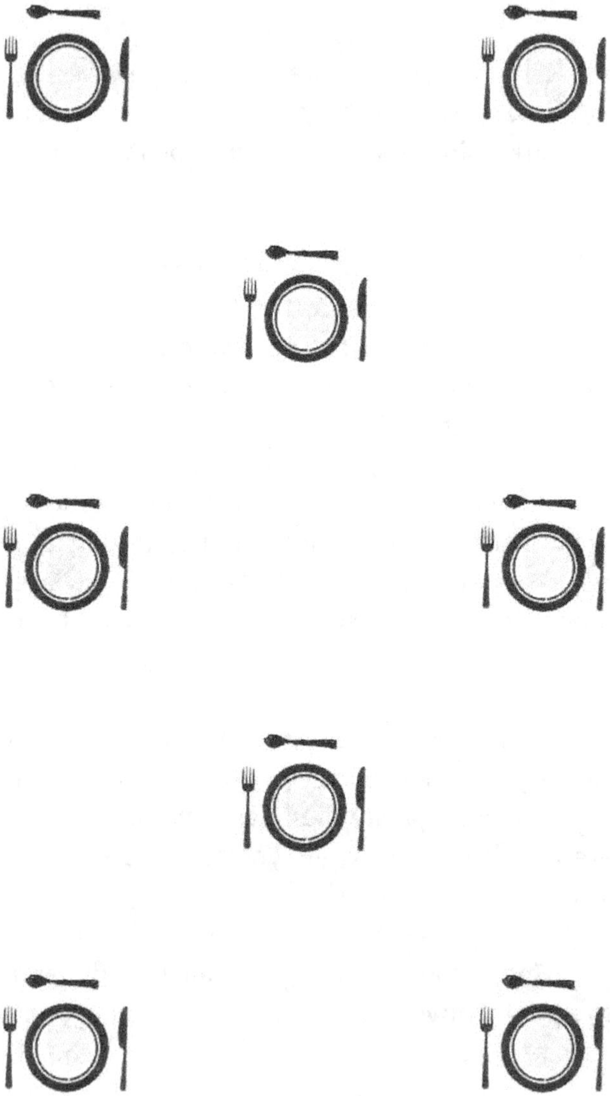

Bibliography

Emerson, Ralph Waldo. Essays and Lectures.

Gymnich, Marion. Lennartz, Norbert: *The Pleasures and Horrors of Eating: The Cultural History of Anglophone Literature (Google EBook)*. Goettingen: V&R Unipress, 2010. Print.

Hitching, Henry. *Sorry!: The English and Their Manners*. New York: Farrar, Strauss and Giroux, 2013. Print.

Jones, Jonathan. *The Guardian*, November 9, London, UK. 2011.

Post, Emely. *Etiquette*. New York, New York: Emely Post, 2014. Print.

Ricotti, Eugenia Prina. "Good and Bad Table Manners in Ancient Greece." Il Punto Di Riferimento per L'archeologia Classica.

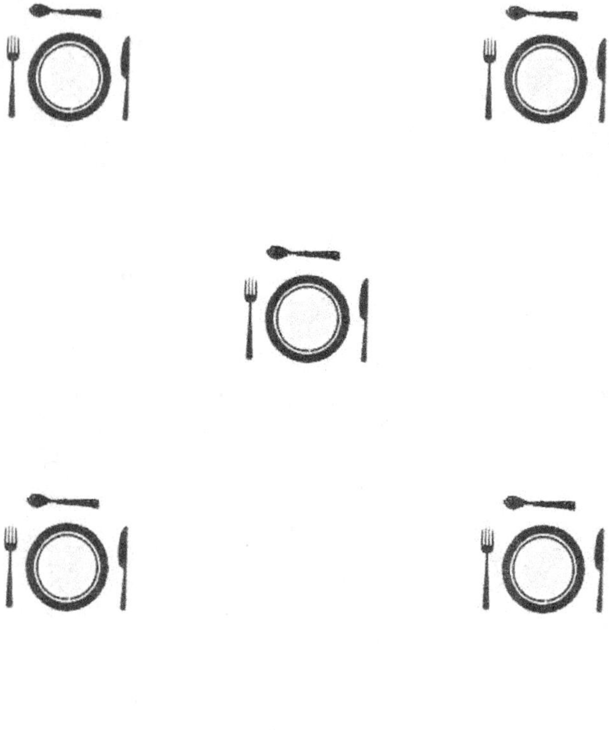

Appendix

Frequently asked Questions

Q: When I find three forks next to each other, which one do I use first?

A: The outer one is always first.

****

Q: Where do I put the used fork when there's more than one?

A: Leave it on the plate or bowl you just used, the waiter will either take it away together, or you hand it to the host when he or she asks for it.

****

Q I hate having a dirty plate in front of me. What do I do with it?

A: Deal with it! Don't push it aside, leave it in front of you until the waiter takes it or the host collects it. It is polite and customary to wait for removal until everyone has finished eating.

Q: I eat with the fork in my right hand, the American way. Sometimes, I just can't get small things, like for example peas, onto my fork. What do I do?

A: Don't push the small stuff around hoping it will eventually make it to your fork. Use a knife or even a small spoon if it is on the table to move these diffi-cult items onto your fork. NEVER use your fingers!

****

Q: I love honey, but it is so messy. I find it impossible to get it to my plate or bread without leaving strings of it on the jar. How do I keep from making a mess?

A: As you lift the honey, twirl it round and round, the tip of the spoon still over the jar, pointing down. It'll stop "stringing". On your plate use a fork to scrape it off the spoon and return the spoon to the honey jar.

****

Q: What is the 10-4 position?

A: Look at the face of a clock. The prongs or tips lean on the 10 o'clock position, the handles rest on the 4 o'clock.

Q: Sometimes, my fork is really full of goop when I'm finished with my meal. How do I clean it?

A: That's easy. Put your fork or your spoon in your mouth as if you were still eating, and pull it out with your lips closed. Guaranteed it will be clean.

****

Q: Sometimes, after cutting something, especially after spreading butter, my knife looks awful with stuff all over it. I know I can't lick it off, so what do I do?

A: Good question! No, never put your knife in your mouth. Slide it vertically along your fork, and it will be nice and clean.

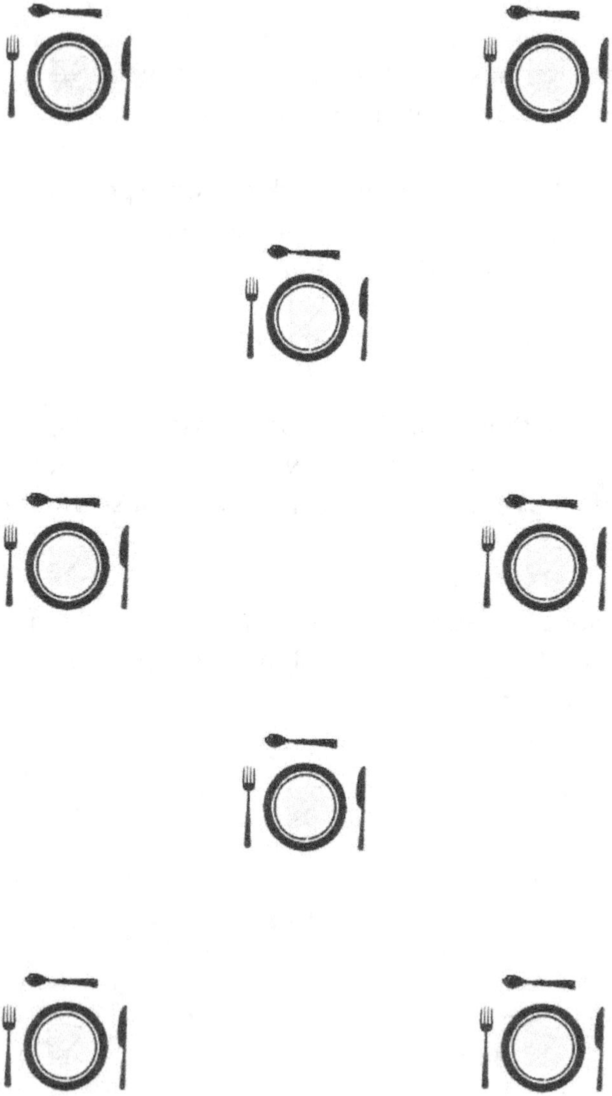

Story of Bravery

*L*et me share a story. Growing up, my family expected that I eat everything whether I liked it or not. The smell, texture and taste of liver made me want to run away from home. No matter what they tried, I couldn't eat liver. Eventually they realized it was hopeless, and served me my favorite, fried eggs.

*N*eedless to say, no liver was ever prepared or allowed in my own home. Then my favorite adopted family invited me to a special dinner. The lady of the house asked my companion, a member of the household, what foods I loved or disliked. "NO LIVER OR OTHER INNARDS PLEASE!"

*Y*ou guessed right. She misunderstood, maybe it was my accent, but she thought liver was my favorite dish and prepared loads of fried liver with onions! My companion wanted to tell her. "She can give you something different." No! Absolutely NO! I would not spoil her pleasure. The platters of fried liver looked ominous.

With great pleasure she placed the largest piece on my plate. I smiled at it, and I swear it smiled back at me. Hurrying, holding my breath and washing each bite down with wine, I got through the liver. Left on my plate were wonderfully delicious vegetables and potatoes.

Our host thought I had gulped the liver because I loved it so much. With even greater pleasure than the first time, she deposited another huge piece on my plate!

And I survived! Making me happy had given her pleasure, and watching her delight made it all worthwhile.

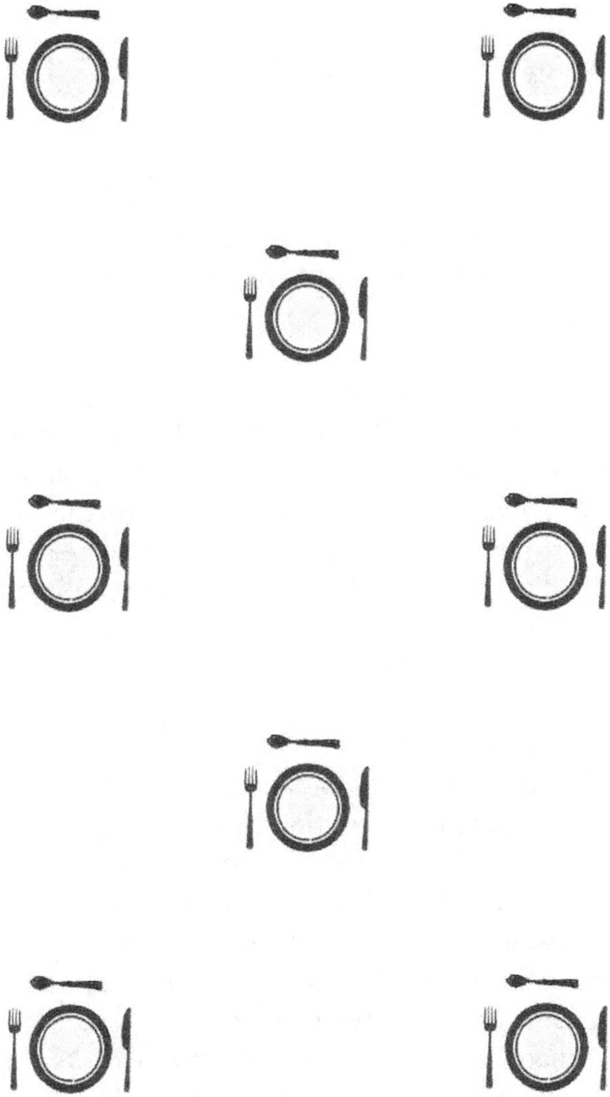

Story of Embarrassment

*L*iving in Florida, I love wearing white clothes in summer. They look and feel cool, they are always stylish. With some nice jewelry, I always felt extremely elegant.

*M*y date invited me to a very elegant restaurant, one with white table cloths and white napkins. It was a wonderful place, one I had visited a number of times. As appetizer we ordered shrimp, the kind that is served with a horseradish-tomato dipping sauce. And of course, that delicious morsel is finger food. You pick up the shrimp by the tail, dip it into the sauce, and lead it to your mouth. Delicious.

*A*fter each shrimp I wiped my hands on my napkin, so I thought. Before picking up my glass for a sip of wine, I reached for that napkin to wipe my mouth. It wasn't there. Where could it be? I looked down and saw that it had slipped off my white slacks and now rested on the floor next to my feet. I had been wiping my hands on my white clothes! Since both napkin and skirt were white, I never noticed that it had fallen. My white clothes were no longer white. Big splotches of red sauce adorned my lap.

I told my date, and we both started to laugh. But inside I was truly mortified, wondering how I would exit through a long room past many diners I knew. I didn't want to leave.

*A*n idea struck me – I asked the waiter for another napkin and discreetly held in in front of me. It didn't work very well, but I felt better, and I walked out with my head held high.

*I*t always pays to be attentive!

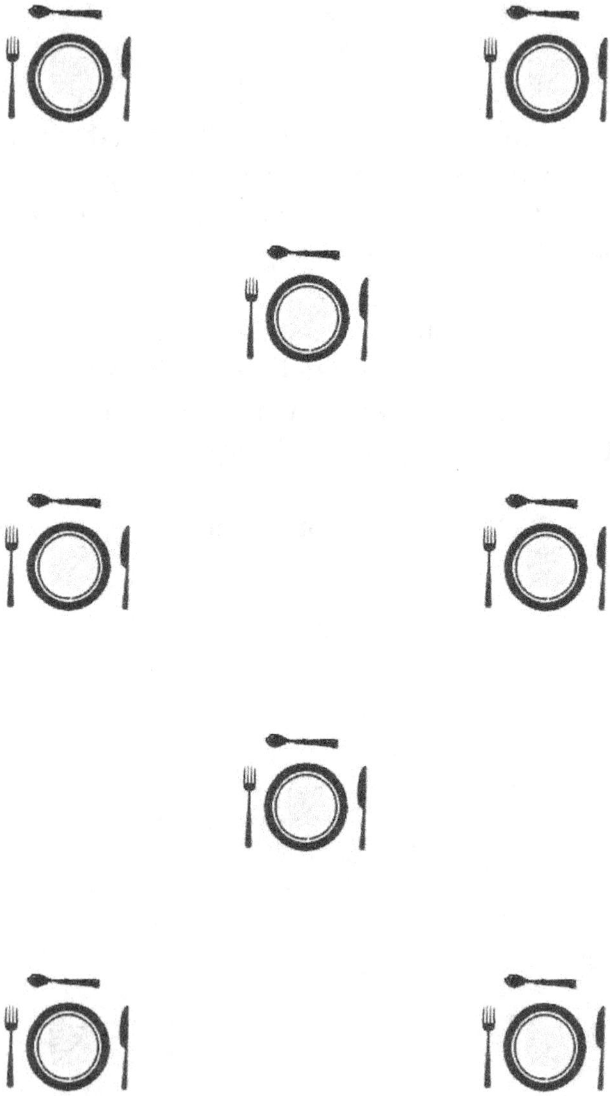

About the Author

Dagmar Pelzer grew up in a family where table manners were drilled and practiced from an early age.

She studied in Germany and the United States, and holds a doctorate in education. She has written teacher training and student materials, has published in professional journals, books, and educational databases, and after retirement started to explore travel writing.

Extensive journeys exposed her to the dining customs of many cultures, and she began to observe the gradual melding and relaxing of the often passionately debated Western table manners.

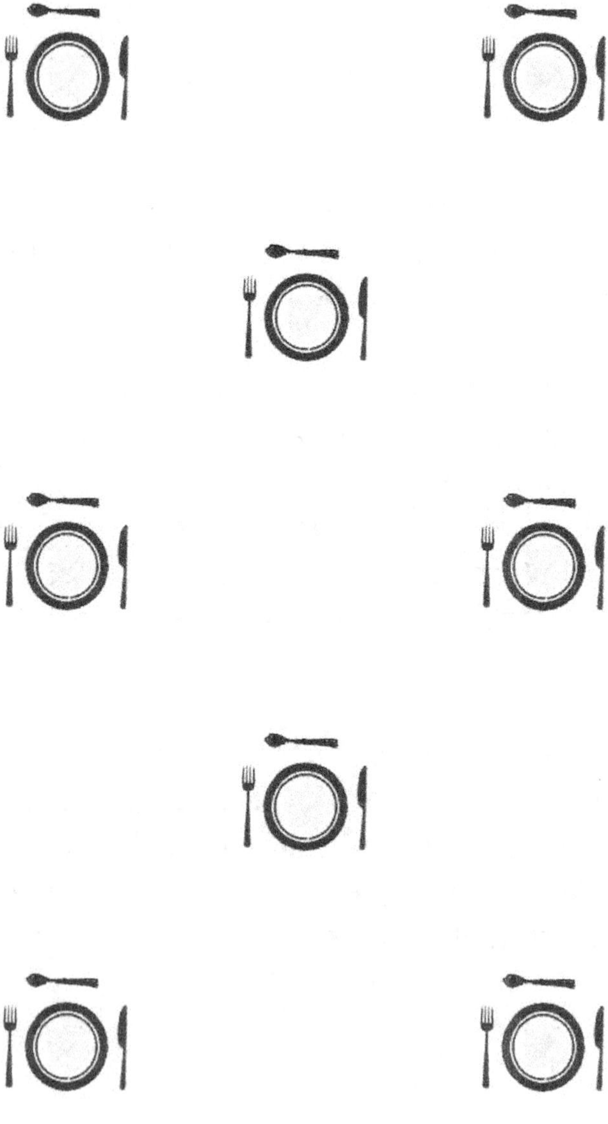

My personal notes

My personal notes

My personal notes

My personal notes

My personal notes

My personal notes

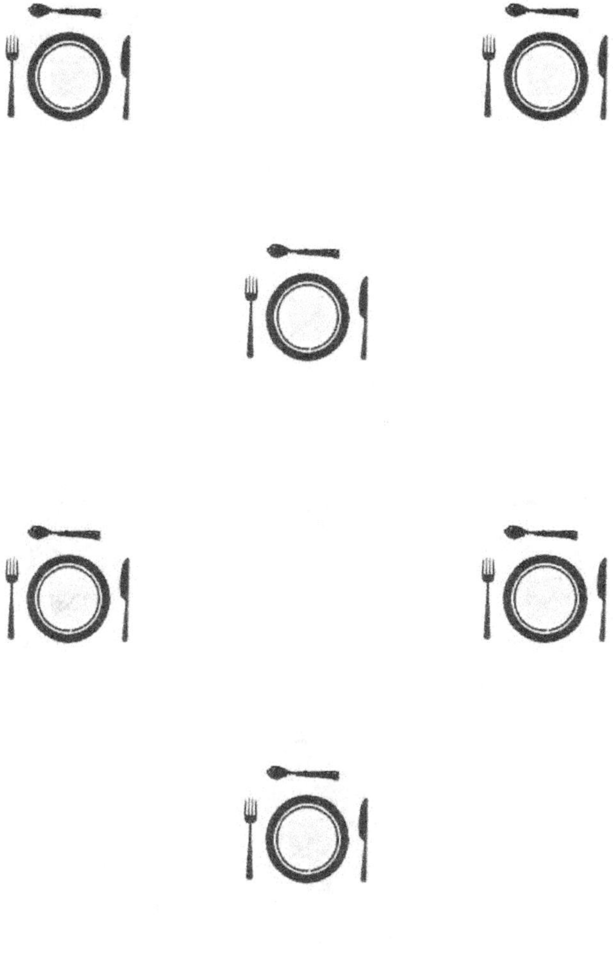

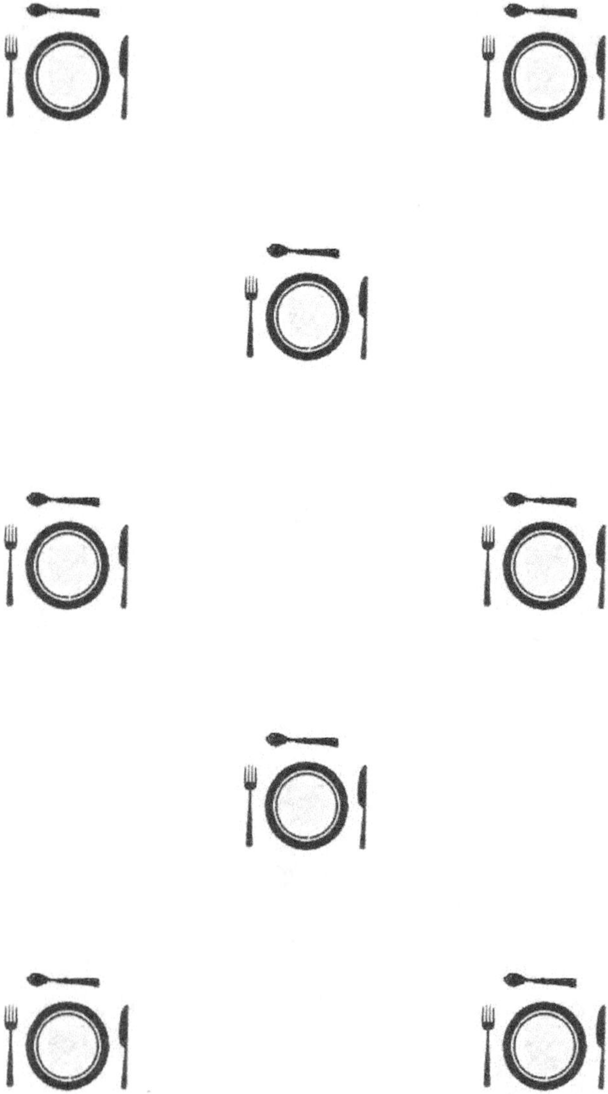

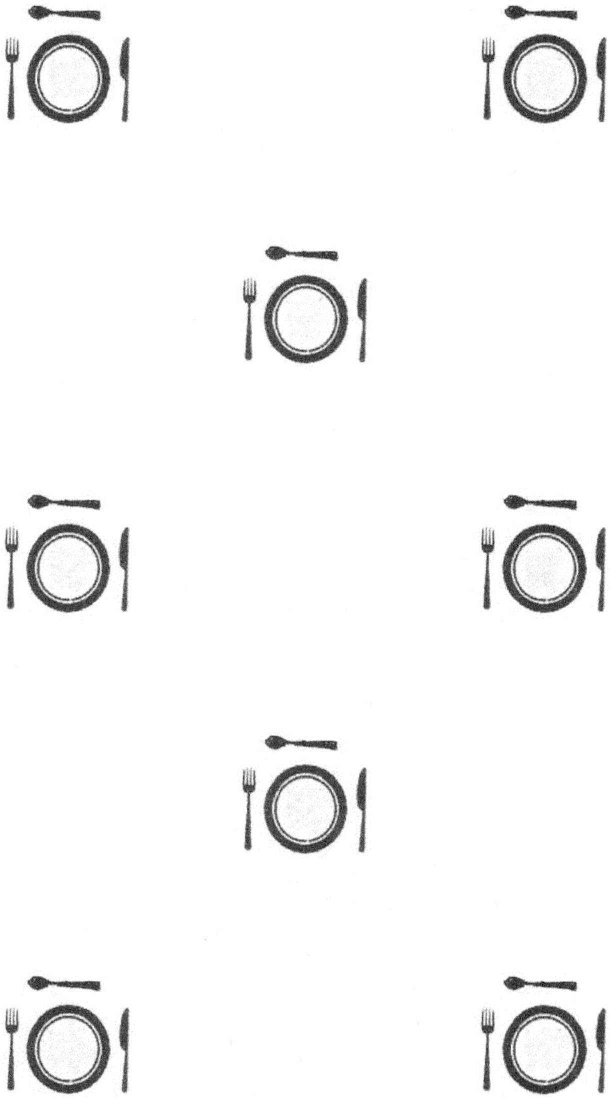

www.ingramcontent.com/pod-product-compliance
Lightning Source LLC
Chambersburg PA
CBHW070426290526
45791CB00005B/1858